God created all things, and all those things were good, but sin entered the world and separated people from God. From the beginning, God was working His plan to make people right with Him again. God sent Jesus to be the perfect payment for sin so that all who repent of their sins and trust Him will be saved. Throughout Scripture, God revealed this plan. He asked His people to trust Him, consistently pointing to Jesus' death, resurrection, and eventual return.

This is that beautiful, grace-filled story.

© 2015 by B&H Publishing Group, Nashville, Tennessee

Scripture quotations are taken from the Holman Christian Standard Bible®, Copyright © 1999, 2000, 2002, 2003, 2009 by Holman Bible Publishers.

Written by Mary Wiley

ISBN: 978-1-4336-8662-7

Dewey Decimal Classification: J226 | Subject Heading: GOSPEL \ JESUS CHRIST \ BIBLE

All rights reserved. Printed in LongGang District, Shenzhen, China, September 2015

2 3 4 5 6 7 8 • 19 18 17 16 15

God Created the World and People Genesis 1-2

In the beginning, there was God the Father, God the Son, and God the Holy Spirit. God was always present and will always be present. He created all things in just six days.

On the first day of creation, God created the heavens and the earth. Then He said "Let there be light!" and there was light! God separated the light and the dark, making day and night. God saw that the light was good. On the second day, God created the sky, and on the third day, God created dry ground between the seas. Each time God spoke, it was as He said.

On the fourth day, God said, "Let there be lights in the sky," and the sun, moon, and stars were created. Then, on the fifth day, God said, "Let the waters be filled with living creatures and the skies filled with birds," and it was so. The sixth day came, and God said, "Let there be many animals on the earth," and it was so. God saw that all He made was good.

Finally, God said, "Let us make man in our image." Man would be deeply loved by God, uniquely made in His image and unlike any other creation. God took dust from the ground and formed a man. He breathed life into the man with His own breath. He named the man Adam. Then God planted a garden in Eden and placed Adam there to care for it. God said, "You may eat from any tree in the garden, but you must not eat from the tree of the knowledge of good and evil. If you eat from that tree, you will die." After this, God saw that Adam needed a helper, so He made a woman from Adam's rib. She was called Eve. God gave Adam and Eve everything they needed, and they only had the one rule God had given Adam. All these things happened on the sixth day, and on the seventh day, God rested from all of His work.

God's Plan for Me: God rules. He created all things and is in control of all things. Why did God create you? Everything was created to give God glory, including you! Giving God glory means to make much of Him or to live in a way that shows how awesome God is. **Revelation 4:11**

Christ Connection: The Bible tells us that God gave Jesus power over creation. All of creation was created through Him, by Him, and for Him. **Colossians 1:15–22**

Noah and the Ark Genesis 6:5-9:17

While Adam and Eve were in the garden, a serpent (who was really Satan), came to them. He asked Eve if God really said that she couldn't eat from one of the trees. The serpent told Eve that she wouldn't die if she ate the fruit—she would be like God! He was very convincing.

Eve ate the fruit God said not to eat, and she gave some to Adam. Adam and Eve had sinned. Because God is just, Adam and Eve's sin would be punished. Eve would have great pain in childbirth and Adam would have to work hard to get food from the ground. They had to leave the garden, and one day, they would die. God showed He still loved them by making clothes for Adam and Eve from the skins of animals before they were sent out. Adam and Eve had many children, and they too were broken by sin.

Generations later, God saw that the people on earth were ruled by sin. Sad that He had made the world, He decided to flood the earth. Everything on earth would die. But God had compassion for a man named Noah and told him to build an ark. Noah was a righteous man who tried to follow God in all things. God promised to keep Noah and his family safe on the ark when the rains came. God also sent pairs of every living thing to the ark so that they would be kept alive too.

Noah, his family, and the animals entered the ark, and God closed the door behind them. It rained for 40 days and 40 nights. The waters covered the earth, and everything on dry land died. When the waters subsided, Noah and his family came out of the ark. Noah built an altar to the Lord and worshiped Him. God put a rainbow in the sky and promised to never flood the whole earth again.

God's Plan for Me: Do you sin? Sin is breaking God's Law, or doing what we want instead of what God wants. We all sin, and Romans 3:23 says the punishment that we deserve for our sin is death and separation from God forever. What are some ways that you have disobeyed God? God asks us to confess our sins. **1 John 1:9**

Christ Connection: God is holy. Sin keeps us from being holy and separates us from God. There's nothing we could do to become holy on our own, so God sent Jesus to live a perfectly holy life so that He could pay for our sins. That way all who love and trust Him could be restored to a right relationship with God. **Romans 6:23**

God Tested Abraham Genesis 22:1-19

God blessed Noah and his family. He told them to have many children so that the earth would be filled with people again.

God formed many nations from these people, one of which would be His people. Abram and Sarai followed God, and they became the beginning of that nation. God spoke to Abram and told him to leave his home and to go to a land that God would show him. He promised that all the people on earth would be blessed through Abram.

Abram obeyed. Then God promised Abram that his children would outnumber the stars in the sky! Abraham did not have any children yet and was very old. Many years passed, and Abram wondered if God would keep His promise. Then God came to Abram again. He changed Abram's name to Abraham and Sarai's name to Sarah. God told Abraham that he would have a son! Sarah heard this and laughed. She thought she was too old to have a baby, but God kept His promise. She had a son that they named Isaac.

When Isaac was older, God asked Abraham to offer him as a sacrifice. A sacrifice is something of great value that is given to God. Usually a sacrifice would be an animal that was killed on an altar, but this time God asked for Abraham's son.

Abraham was sad, but He trusted God. He took Isaac up the mountain and tied him to the altar. Just as he was about to do as God had asked, the angel of the Lord stopped him. Abraham saw a ram caught in the bushes. God had provided a sacrifice! The angel of the Lord promised that God would bless Abraham and make his family great. God kept all of His promises to Abraham's family.

God's Plan for Me: God provided Jesus to be the sacrifice in our place. Our sin deserved death, but Jesus took our punishment on the cross. There's nothing we can do to earn forgiveness. Jesus' sacrifice was a free gift. Have you ever tried to earn God's favor by being good? Why doesn't that work? **2 Corinthians 5:21; Ephesians 2:8–9**

Christ Connection: God provided the ram as a substitute for Isaac. Similarly, God provided a perfect substitute for us through Jesus. Jesus took our place on the cross and the punishment that we deserved for sin so that we could have His place of righteousness before God. **1 John 4:10**

Stolen Blessing   Genesis 25:27-34; 27:1-45

God remembered His promise to make Abraham's descendants outnumber the stars. Isaac married a woman named Rebekah who was unable to have children. Isaac and Rebekah prayed and prayed that God would give them children, and one day Rebekah had twins! It was a miracle! God told Rebekah, "The babies in your womb will become two nations. One people will be stronger than the other, and the older will serve the younger."

Esau was born first, then Jacob. Esau became a hunter, and Jacob worked at home. One day, Esau came home from hunting and was very tired. Jacob was cooking a stew, and Esau asked to have some. Jacob told Esau that he would give him some stew, but only if Esau gave up his birthright. A birthright was a promise that the family's wealth would one day belong to Esau. Esau was so hungry that he gave that right away.

Later, when Isaac was very old, it was time to give a blessing to Esau. Jacob disguised himself and tricked Isaac into giving him the blessing that was meant for Esau! When Esau returned, he was angry and wanted to kill Jacob, so Jacob went to live with relatives.

Jacob lived far from home for many years. He had wives, children, and livestock. Then one day God told him to go back home. Jacob went, but he was afraid Esau would still be angry with him. One night on the way, God wrestled Jacob, and at daybreak God blessed him and changed his name to Israel.

Esau met Jacob before he got home. He treated Jacob kindly, and their families settled together. God's promise to Abraham would continue through Jacob. His family would be God's people. They would be called Israelites.

God's Plan for Me: Jacob sinned by tricking his brother and deceiving his father. Sin separates us from God, but it doesn't surprise God when we mess up. God knew Jacob would sin, but He still loved Jacob and planned to send Jesus through Jacob's family. Could you ever do something so bad that it would make God stop loving you? Is anyone unable to be forgiven by God? **Romans 8:38-39**

Christ Connection: Jacob is a perfect example of why a Savior was needed. Like Jacob, we seek a birthright and blessing that is not ours, but we cannot lie, deceive, or trick to receive God's blessing. Jesus shared His birthright and blessing with us when He paid for our sins on the cross and gave us His righteousness. **Galatians 3:29**

Joseph's Dreams Came True Genesis 41:53–46:34; 50:15-21

Jacob had twelve sons, but Joseph was his favorite. Jacob even gave Joseph a special coat of many colors to wear. This made Joseph's brothers very angry. To add to their anger, Joseph told them about two of his dreams. In both, the brothers bowed down before Joseph and served him. The brothers didn't want this to happen. They plotted to kill Joseph. They threw him into a pit, but then a group of people came that was on the way to Egypt. They bought Joseph as a slave. The brothers told their father that Joseph had been killed by a wild animal, and their father was very sad.

However, God was with Joseph. Joseph was put in charge of a household, but then he was thrown in jail for something he did not do. Even in jail, God blessed Joseph by helping him interpret dreams. Joseph interpreted a dream for the pharaoh's cupbearer, who told the pharaoh about Joseph. Before long, Joseph was interpreting dreams for Pharaoh too!

Pharaoh's dream meant that there would be a famine in the land for seven years. Because God gave Joseph the ability to interpret this dream, he was able to make a plan for all of Egypt to have enough food for those seven years. The pharaoh was pleased and put Joseph in charge of all of Egypt, second only to Pharaoh.

When the famine became bad in the land, Joseph's brothers came to him because they were in need of food. They did not recognize Joseph. They bowed before him, as his dream had foretold many years before. Joseph told them, "Don't be afraid. You planned evil against me, but God used it to bring about great good." He told the brothers to go get Jacob and all of their families. Joseph promised to care for them in Egypt. He would make sure they all had enough food during the famine, and that his family would continue in Egypt for many years.

God's Plan for Me: Joseph was not perfect, but he had not done anything to deserve the evil his brothers did to him. Jesus was perfect and undeserving of the punishment He endured for the sins of all people. Have you ever been punished for something you didn't do? Jesus willingly went to the cross so that we could be made right before God! **Isaiah 53:5**

Christ Connection: God used the evil done to Joseph for good. One day, Jesus would come through Joseph's family. Those who crucified Jesus intended it for evil, but God's plan was for Him to be the way that all who trust Him might be made righteous. All who call on Jesus will be saved! **Romans 10:13**

The Israelites Crossed the Red Sea Exodus 13:17–17:7

Joseph died, and many years passed. A new pharaoh came to power who didn't know about the great things Joseph had done. Instead, he was afraid that Joseph's family would take over Egypt, so he made them slaves. Pharaoh also made a law that all of the Israelite baby boys must be thrown into the Nile River.

One mom didn't want this to happen to her son, so she put him in a basket, hoping someone would save him. Pharaoh's daughter did just that when she found him. She named the baby Moses.

Moses grew up, and one day God spoke to him from a burning bush and told him to lead His people out of slavery in Egypt. Moses went to Pharaoh, but Pharaoh refused to let the people go. Then God showed His power by sending plagues to convince Pharaoh to let God's people go. All Egyptians lost their firstborn sons and the firstborn males of all their flocks in the last plague, and there was much sorrow in the land. Pharaoh became afraid of what else might happen and told the Israelites to leave immediately!

The Lord led His people toward the Red Sea, but Pharaoh changed his mind and sent his army to bring back the people. The Israelites were scared. How would they get away? God was with His people. He parted the sea, and the Israelites crossed on dry ground! The water closed behind them, and the Egyptian army was drowned in the water.

God led the Israelites in a pillar of cloud by day and fire by night. After three months, God spoke to Moses, "If you listen to Me and keep My covenant, you will be My people." Later, God returned to Moses in a cloud of thunder and lightning and gave him the Ten Commandments to help His people know how to live. God knew they would not be able to keep these Laws perfectly, so He made a system for them to sacrifice animals once a year to God to pay for their sins. Even though God's people frequently turned away from Him, God continued to be faithful to His people.

God's Plan for Me: God rescued His people from Egypt and taught them how to live in a way that honors Him. God gave us the Bible so that we can know all He has done for us and how we can live to give glory to Him. What have you learned from the Bible? How can you learn more about what God wants us to do? **2 Timothy 3:16–17**

Christ Connection: God saved Moses for a special purpose: to rescue His people. The last plague is called the death of the firstborn, and it is a picture of the payment required for sin, which is death. This event would be remembered every year by God's people because God spared them from the judgment that the Egyptians experienced. Through Jesus, we are rescued from our sin and made God's people. **1 Peter 3:18**

Joshua and Caleb — Numbers 13:1–14:38

After a long journey from Egypt, the Israelites finally reached Canaan, which was the land God promised them. God told them to send twelve men into the land to see it. Moses did what God asked and told the men to be bring back fruit from the land. Forty days later, the men returned carrying a cluster of grapes that was so big it had to be carried on a pole by two men! The land was a good land!

Instead of being excited about this land, the Israelites were sad. They knew the land was good but thought that the people who lived in Canaan were too powerful to beat in battle. They thought they had made the long trip for no reason.

Only Joshua and Caleb trusted that God would give them the land He had promised. They told the people that there was no reason to be afraid because God was with them, but the people wouldn't listen. God was angry and punished them for not trusting Him. His people would spend 40 years wandering the wilderness, and only Joshua and Caleb would get to enter Canaan because they had trusted God.

Even in the wilderness, God showed His mercy to His people. God gave them water from a rock, food to eat, and made their clothes so that they would not wear out. Still the people grumbled. God was angry, so He sent snakes among them. Many people died.

Moses asked God to take the snakes away, and God told him to make a snake image and put it on a pole. Moses did as God asked, and anyone who looked at the snake after being bitten was healed! Again God showed mercy in the wilderness even after His people had sinned. He provided a way for them to be healed.

Years later, God's people were brought into the Promised Land. God had kept His promise! He gave them favor in battle and delivered the land over to them.

God's Plan for Me: The Israelites forgot how the Lord had provided for them and didn't trust Him to take them into the Promised Land. Are there times that you forget that God always keeps His promises? What does it mean for you to trust God? **Deuteronomy 7:9**

Christ Connection: Sin created a huge problem for the Israelites. Because of our sin, we face a huge problem: we are separated from God. We deserve to die. The bronze snake was an example of what Jesus would be for us: anyone who looks to Jesus on the cross and trusts in Him will be saved and be made right with God. **John 3:14–15**

David and Goliath 1 Samuel 16-17

Not too long after God's people entered Canaan, Joshua died. Without Joshua to remind them of their commitment to God, they began to disobey Him and worship idols. God was angry and allowed other nations to attack them. After being ruled by another nation for many years, the Israelites cried out to God and turned from their sins. God raised up a judge to lead them. Then Israel would repeat the same pattern: they would disobey God, cry out in repentance, and another new judge would be raised up.

After being ruled by judges for many years, the Israelites demanded a king so that they could be like the nations around them. They forgot that God was their ultimate King.

Saul became Israel's first king, but Saul did not obey God. God rejected Saul as king and chose a new king, but the change of power didn't happen immediately. God's new king was named David. He was the youngest of eight sons and a shepherd.

Around this time, the Philistines were getting ready to attack Israel. Saul sent his army to them. Goliath was a Philistine warrior who was 9 feet 9 inches tall! He wanted Israel to send their best man for him to fight one-on-one, but no one wanted to fight him!

David went to check on his brothers who were in the Israelite army. While there, David decided that he would fight Goliath. The armor offered to him was too big. He took only his slingshot and five stones. Goliath laughed at David, but David said, "You fight with a spear and a sword, but I fight in the name of God!" David took out a stone, slung it, and hit Goliath in the forehead. Goliath fell facedown and was defeated.

After David killed Goliath, he went to live in Saul's palace. David became best friends with Saul's son, Jonathan. Saul was jealous of David and planned to kill him, but Jonathan helped him escape. Despite this, David did become king one day. God promised David that future kings of Israel would come from his family. God was continuing the promise He made to Abraham, and one day Jesus would come from David's family.

God's Plan for Me: The Israelites repented of their sins and turned back to God many times, but they would often fall back into sin. What does it mean to repent? When we repent from our sins, we confess them to God and turn away from sin and to Him. When we follow Jesus, we will still sin, but God wants us to turn away from that sin and to Him. God wants us to think about all the good things that He has done for us and to worship Him! **Acts 3:19**

Christ Connection: The Israelites didn't stand a chance against Goliath, their toughest enemy, but God gave David power to defeat him! David reminds us of Jesus, who came to save us from our greatest enemies: sin and death. Jesus is our ultimate Hero and the perfect King. He gives salvation and eternal life. **Romans 10:9-10**

Isaiah Preached about the Messiah   Isaiah 53

Many years passed, and many kings ruled the Israelites. Some kings were good and some were evil, but all sinned and faced the consequences of those sins. Israel continued their pattern of sin, crying out to God, and turning back to Him. God sent prophets to remind Israel of all His goodness and their need to turn back to Him. The prophets told God's people of the dangers of living in a way that didn't please Him and what would happen in the future, but God's people didn't always understand the prophets' teaching.

God spoke through the prophet Isaiah to tell His people to turn back to God, but they did not listen. Even though the people were far from God, He told Isaiah that some of the Israelites would be His people again. God promised that He would send a Messiah who would pay for the sins of people and that anyone who loved and trusted Him would be made right before God. God said that men would reject the Messiah and that He would be pierced because of our sins. This Messiah would be perfectly innocent but would die to pay for sin. God used the prophets to give hope to His people, and after waiting for hundreds of years, all that Isaiah said came true.

The time between Isaiah's prophecies about Jesus and His birth was about 700 years. That's a long time to wait, but God kept the promises He had made about Jesus. Jesus would not be the king that God's people had expected or asked for; He would be better.

God's Plan for Me: Why do we need a Savior? Just like Israel sinned, we sin. Our sin separates us from God, and there's nothing we can do to have a right relationship with Him. Only Jesus could do something about this separation. Jesus came so that we might have salvation and eternal life, by giving us His place before God. **Acts 4:12**

Christ Connection: God's plan to save His people from sin and death was not a secret plan. Although the disobedience of God's people seemed too big of a problem, God had an even bigger solution. The prophets told Israel that a Savior was coming who would set them free, not from the hard times they faced, but from sin! This is Jesus, who would come to make all things right and give forgiveness to any who trust Him. **Isaiah 61:1–2; Luke 4:18–19**

Angels Spoke to Mary and Joseph   Luke 1:26-56; Matthew 1:18-24

For hundreds of years, God's people waited for a Messiah. It had been 400 years since God had spoken through one of His prophets, and it seemed God had become silent. And then God sent an angel to speak to Mary about what was about to happen.

Mary lived in Nazareth and was engaged to Joseph, a man from the family of King David, when Gabriel, an angel of the Lord, came to her. He said, "Rejoice! You have found favor with God. He is with you. Don't be afraid, Mary. You will have a son, and you will name Him Jesus. He will be great, and He will be called the Son of the Most High. God will give Him the throne of David, and His kingdom will never end."

"How can this be?" Mary asked. "I am not married yet."

Gabriel answered, "The Holy Spirit will come upon you, and God will be the child's father. He will be called the Son of God. Remember your relative Elizabeth? She was childless but is now going to have a son. Nothing is impossible with God."

Mary answered, "I belong to God. Let everything happen as you said." Then the angel left her.

When Joseph found out Mary was pregnant, he decided to divorce her quietly. Then an angel appeared to Joseph and told him not to be afraid to take Mary as his wife. The angel said the baby was from God and they should name Him Jesus. He would save people from their sins. Joseph believed it all and took Mary as his wife.

After the angel left Mary, she went to see her cousin Elizabeth. When Mary entered the house, the baby inside Elizabeth, who was John the Baptist, leaped with joy. Elizabeth and the baby inside her recognized that the baby Mary would soon have was the Son of God! John the Baptist would grow up to tell many people about this miraculous Jesus who was to be born soon to Mary.

God's Plan for Me: Has anyone ever told you about something that would happen soon that made you very excited? Maybe you were going on a trip or having a new baby in your family. Jesus' birth was the biggest and best announcement that we could ever receive! From the beginning of time, Jesus had been the plan to save God's people from their sin, and He was finally here! **Isaiah 9:6**

Christ Connection: The baby Jesus fulfilled Isaiah's prophecy as well as other prophecies of the coming Savior throughout the Old Testament. Through His life, death, and resurrection, Jesus fulfilled God's plan of redemption that God planned from the beginning of the world. **Isaiah 7:14**

Jesus Was Born Luke 2:1-20

When Mary was pregnant with Jesus, the Roman emperor ordered everyone to be registered for a census. Every person traveled to the town where his family was from to be counted. Because Joseph was from the family of King David, he and Mary left Nazareth and went to Bethlehem. They needed a place to stay, but the only room left was where the animals were kept. It was time for Mary to have her baby, so there Jesus was born. Mary wrapped Him in cloth and laid Him in a feeding trough.

There were shepherds in a field nearby who were watching their flocks because it was night. Suddenly an angel of the Lord stood before them, and a bright light shone around them. They were terrified! The angel said, "Don't be afraid! I bring you good news of great joy! Today a Savior, who is Messiah the Lord, was born for you in the city of David. You will find Him wrapped in cloth and lying in a feeding trough." Then the sky was filled with angels praising God and saying, "Glory to God in the highest heaven, and peace on earth to people He favors."

The shepherds hurried off to Bethlehem to see this Baby. There they found Mary and Joseph with Jesus, who was lying in a trough, just as the angel had said. The shepherds returned to their fields, praising God for all they had seen and heard.

When Jesus was a little older, wise men came from far away in the east to worship Him. They had seen a star that led them to Bethlehem. They asked King Herod where the King of the Jews had been born. This upset Herod. He wanted to be the only king. Herod plotted to kill Jesus but did not know where He was.

The wise men went along their way, and the star led them right to Jesus' house. They brought Him gifts of gold, frankincense, and myrrh and fell to their knees to worship Him. Mary and Joseph later moved to Egypt so that Jesus would be kept safe. After Herod died, they returned to Israel, and Jesus grew up.

God's Plan for Me: God sent Jesus to be born into the world as a baby so that He would live a perfect life that we couldn't live and be the righteous sacrifice required to pay for our sins. God's love for us is so great that He was willing to send His only begotten Son to die on the cross to bring salvation to the world. How does it make you feel to know how much God must love you for this to be true? **John 3:16–18**

Christ Connection: Jesus had been born just as the prophets said He would. Jesus was not an ordinary baby. He was God's Son, sent to earth from heaven. Jesus came into the world to save people from their sins and to be their King. **Galatians 4:4–5**

Jesus and John the Baptist   John 3:22-36

Jesus grew in wisdom and stature, and in favor with God and people. When the time came for Him to begin His earthly ministry, He went to John the Baptist. John was baptizing people in the Jordan River as they confessed their sins. John had been teaching that the Lord was coming and the kingdom of heaven was near. Jesus went to see John because He wanted to be baptized by him. But John didn't think he should baptize Jesus. "I need to be baptized by you," John told Jesus.

Jesus answered him, "Do this because this is what the Lord wants." John did as Jesus asked. He baptized Jesus. As Jesus came up out of the water, the heavens were torn open and the Holy Spirit came down on Jesus like a dove. A voice from heaven said, "This is My beloved Son. I take great joy in Him!"

Then Jesus was led by the Holy Spirit into the wilderness to be tempted by the devil. For forty days and forty nights, Jesus fasted. This means that Jesus did not eat any food during that time. He was very hungry! The devil knew Jesus was hungry, and he came to Jesus and said, "If You are the Son of God, tell this stone to become bread." But Jesus answered, "It is written: Man must not live on bread alone but on every word that comes from the mouth of God."

Then the devil led Jesus to the top of the temple to tempt Him. The devil asked Jesus to prove He was God's Son by jumping off the temple and seeing if angels would catch Him. But Jesus said, "It is also written: Do not test the Lord your God."

Again the devil tempted Jesus. He showed Him all the kingdoms of the world and promised all of them to Jesus if He would worship the devil. Jesus said, "Go away, Satan! It is written: Worship the Lord your God, and serve only Him." After the devil had finished every temptation and still Jesus had not sinned, he left Jesus for a time, and the angels came and began to serve Jesus.

God's Plan for Me: The devil tried to trick Jesus into sinning, just like he had done to Adam and Eve in the Garden of Eden, but Jesus was perfect. He did not fall to any of the temptations that the devil offered. Instead, He responded with Scripture, quieting the devil and showing that Jesus was far more powerful than the devil. How can you respond to temptation like Jesus did? Why does it matter that Jesus was sinless?
Psalm 119:9; 1 Corinthians 15:57

Christ Connection: Jesus responded to the devil's tempting with Scripture and unwavering faith. Although Jesus faced temptation, He never sinned. Jesus came to redeem those who had tried to beat temptation by following all of God's rules and failed. Jesus was perfect and righteous. A perfect sacrifice was required to pay for sin. Jesus was that perfect sacrifice for us when He died on the cross. **John 1:17; Romans 5:6**

The Sermon on the Mount   Matthew 5–7

Jesus did not fall to temptation, which proved that He was the perfect Son of God. After His temptation, He traveled to Galilee and preached the good news of God. He was talking about Himself and what He would do for all people. "The kingdom of God has come near," He said. "Repent—turn away from your sins—and believe in the good news."

As Jesus walked near the Sea of Galilee, He saw Simon Peter and Andrew, who were fisherman. He said to them, "Follow Me, and I will teach you to fish for people!" The brothers left their work and followed Him. Jesus called many other disciples as well: James and his brother John, Matthew, Philip, Bartholomew, Matthew, Thomas, James the son of Alphaeus, Thaddaeus, Simon the Zealot, and Judas Iscariot, who would one day betray Jesus. All of the disciples left their work and their families to follow Jesus.

Jesus traveled all over Galilee, Judea, and Samaria teaching about the Kingdom of God and the forgiveness of sins that was available to people through His coming death and resurrection for all who would trust Him. His disciples traveled with Him, and they were amazed at what Jesus taught. His teachings were different than the teaching they normally heard in the synagogues. He taught with God's authority about how to live, how to treat each other, and how to love God.

Jesus also performed many miracles so that people would believe that He was the Messiah. He healed the sick, caused the blind to see, and even raised people from the dead. He drove out demons, fed more than 5,000 people with just two fish and five small loaves of bread, and calmed a storm. Many times He not only healed people but also told them their sins had been forgiven! This was something that only God could do. Jesus was God's Son who had all authority, and He knew that He would soon pay for sin on the cross. Some people were angry that Jesus claimed to forgive sin and taught things that were not like what they had always heard, so they plotted to kill Jesus. But others did believe and became Christians.

God's Plan for Me: Jesus declared many people's sins forgiven when He saw that they had faith in Him. His teaching was so great that many were amazed, confused, or doubtful that it was the truth. What questions do you have about Jesus or His teachings? Do you believe that what the Bible says about Jesus is true? **Romans 5:8**

Christ Connection: Jesus came to save people from their sin. Until Jesus' death and resurrection, God's people made a sacrifice once a year to God so that their sins would be forgiven. The priest would speak to God for the people. Jesus taught a new way because He would be the perfect sacrifice to pay for sin on the cross, and this way also allowed us to draw near to God. **Hebrews 7:18–19**

Jesus' Crucifixion and Resurrection Matthew 26:36–28:10

Jesus traveled to Jerusalem so that all that was written about Him would be fulfilled. He entered the city as if He were a king! He rode on a donkey, and a large crowd spread their robes on the road in front of Him. They shouted, "The King who comes in the name of the Lord is the blessed One. Peace in heaven and glory in the highest heaven!" Many in the crowd believed Jesus was the promised King, but some were plotting against Him.

The Passover was approaching. This was a day when God's people ate a meal together to remember when God brought them out of slavery in Egypt and took them to the Promised Land. Jesus ate this Passover meal with His disciples. This wasn't a normal Passover meal though. Jesus said that all future Passover meals would be done to remember His death that offered forgiveness of sins.

After dinner, Jesus and the disciples went to the Garden of Gethsemane. Jesus knew what was about to happen. He went to pray alone and fell to the ground, "Father, if it is possible, let this cup of suffering pass from me. But Your will be done." He returned to His disciples, and soon a crowd led by Judas came carrying swords and clubs. The crowd arrested Him, and His disciples ran away.

The leaders of the temple said Jesus spoke against God, but the Roman governor didn't think Jesus had done anything wrong. He tried to release Jesus, but the crowd yelled for Him to be crucified. Jesus was mocked and beaten and then nailed to a cross. During Jesus' last three hours on the cross, darkness covered the land. Then Jesus cried out to God and died. The earth quaked, and the veil in the temple was torn in two.

Jesus' body was placed in a tomb with a big stone at the entrance. Three days later, an angel of the Lord rolled the stone away, and Jesus walked from the tomb. Jesus was alive! He had risen from the dead, just as He said He would!

God's Plan for Me: Through Jesus' death we have forgiveness of sins, and through His resurrection we have a promise of eternal life with Him for all who believe. Jesus died on the cross in our place so that our sins could be forgiven. When we love and trust Jesus, we get credit for His perfect life as a free gift to us! This is the most valuable gift we could ever receive! How would you react to a great gift? How should we respond to the gift that Jesus has given us? **John 15:13**

Christ Connection: The crucifixion and resurrection of Jesus is the center of the gospel. We deserve to die because of our sin, but Jesus died in our place. He was the blood sacrifice made once and for all for the forgiveness of sin. God was pleased with Jesus' sacrifice and raise Jesus from the dead to reign as King over all creation. We are forgiven only through Jesus. **John 3:16–18; Acts 4:12**

Jesus Appeared to the Disciples

Mark 16:14; Luke 24:36-43; John 20:19-29; Acts 1:3

Shortly after Jesus' resurrection, He joined two disciples when they were walking on the road toward Emmaus. The two did not recognize Him and were talking about what had happened with Jesus. He explain that all had happened to fulfill what the prophets had said about Him. When the two finally realized they were talking with Jesus, He disappeared from their sight. They rushed away to tell the other disciples.

The disciples were hiding in a house because they were afraid they might be made to suffer like Jesus because they were His followers. Then, suddenly, Jesus was standing among them! The disciples were terrified! But Jesus answered, "Why are you troubled? Look at My Hands and My feet. It is I!" The disciples were overjoyed! Jesus had risen from the dead!

Jesus spent forty days on earth after His resurrection and appeared to more than 500 people. Jesus told them, "Go into all the world and tell the good news about Me to all people. Make disciples of all nations and baptize them in the name of the Father and of the Son and of the Holy Spirit. Teach them to obey everything I have commanded you. I will be with you." Jesus also told His disciples that He was going to ascend to heaven, but He would send the Holy Spirit to be with them and with all who trust Him. Then Jesus rose up into the sky, and a cloud took Him out of their sight. An angel appeared and told them that Jesus had been taken into heaven and would come again. Jesus would come again in the same way He went up into heaven. All that Jesus had said happened.

God's Plan for Me: God cares so deeply for you that He was willing to send His Son, Jesus, to die on the cross for sin. Then God brought Him back to life! Why is it important that Jesus rose again? God showed us that He accepted Jesus' sacrifice for our sins through Jesus' resurrection and that He gives us the promise of eternal life. **1 Corinthians 6:14**

Christ Connection: The good news about what Jesus has done to rescue us from our sins is too great to keep to ourselves. Before Jesus went back to heaven, He gave the disciples a job to do. Jesus wants His followers to teach people everywhere about Him. **1 Corinthians 15:1-7**

Jesus Christ Will Return Revelation 19-22

After Jesus ascended into heaven, the Holy Spirit came, and the church grew. Word spread about Jesus, and many believed! Still others opposed the church's growth. Generations and generations of people were born and died. This is where we enter the story. Jesus promised that He would return one day, just as He had gone into heaven.

God gave John a vision of heaven and showed him what would happen when Jesus comes back to earth. He saw the heavens open and Jesus on a white horse. He was wearing a robe stained with blood, His eyes were like fire, and He wore many crowns. An army wearing white linen followed Him. Satan, who was seen as a beast, waged war against the rider but did not win. He was thrown into the lake of fire. Then there was a new heaven and a new earth.

When that day comes, God's glory will shine so brightly that there will be no need for the sun or moon. God will live with man. They will be His people, and He will be their God. He will wipe away every tear from their eyes. Death, sadness, and pain will no longer exist, and God's people will be with Him forever and ever.

God's Plan for Me: Now that you've finished the story, how can you respond? You can respond by understanding who God is (a holy God) and who you are (a sinner). Pray and tell God you know you have sinned and that you want Him to be the one that leads your life. Turn away from your sin and to Jesus, trusting only in Him to save you. You can know that God will always be with you through the Holy Spirit and you will go to heaven when you die. Your sins are forgiven and you are a Christian and a child of God! Then, you will want to tell others about this decision. Talk with an adult about getting baptized to show that you are a follower of Jesus, and find a church to be a part of so that the people there can help you follow Jesus.

You can learn more about Jesus and how to live for God by reading the Bible and talking to Him every day. Ask God to help you live for Him. Thank God for saving you through Jesus!

Write below about the decision you have made:
_____
_____
_____

Christ Connection: Jesus promised to come back to earth soon. When He returns, those who know and love Jesus will be with Him and enjoy Him forever. God will undo every bad thing caused by sin. There will be no more death, no more pain, and no more tears. Jesus will make all things new. **Revelation 21:5**